W9-BIL-880

Bunker, Robert   etal

The first look at strangers

DATE DUE			
FEB. 8			

The First Look at Strangers

THE FIRST LOOK AT STRANGERS

ROBERT BUNKER

•

JOHN ADAIR

RUTGERS UNIVERSITY PRESS

New Brunswick   *New Jersey*

1959

Contents

Acknowledgments

※

Dr. Alexander H. Leighton, creator of the seminar here described, has asked that we acknowledge for him the very generous help it received. In particular, United States Indian Service employees both in the field and in Washington offered assistance without which there could have been no seminar; their willingness to serve as targets of critical examination proved their real desire to have others learn by their experience. Department of Agriculture officials in Washington, Flagstaff, and Santa Fe aided in planning, lent quarters, and helped the seminar set up in Truchas. The Museum of Anthropology in Santa Fe provided office space all one summer. The Carnegie Corporation of New York and the Russell Sage Foundation provided financial support and their officers' encouragement, over as many years as the seminar staff felt necessary for inquiry into and demonstration of the principles detailed in the pages that follow.

R. B.
J. A.

The First Look at Strangers

Introduction

Into a New Land

The dozen students in the cars were administrators and resource technicians, men and women with working experience in their fields. Their teachers were anthropologists from Cornell and the University of Arizona.

They drove up over the hill from the Indian Agency and past the clutter of outlying houses. The students looked almost longingly at the big, barnlike trading post, one last familiar landmark. In a few minutes now, each would be on his own, to make what he could of the Papagos and their arid land.

They scanned the horizons furiously, trying to tie what they saw to what they had been told in their two days' briefing. Yes, the Papagos had some few acres in irrigated pasture. And all around lay cactus desert, stretching long miles toward blue, jagged peaks. One car stopped at a small mud-brick house. A student stepped out. The others watched while he knocked at a door and waited; no one came. He tried again at the door of a shed, then walked uncertainly toward the branch-work summer shelter (the ramada), behind. At last he waved, and his fellows drove on. The teacher at the wheel stopped next at a small Papago village; he stopped again down the road. One by one his students headed out, to learn what they could learn.

They had known that they might feel foolish, at least while they were making first contacts and sizing up whatever Papagos they met, figuring out where conversation might best begin. They had expected their feeling of shyness, nakedness almost, of losing all social bearings. What they had not foreseen was their sense of impersonality. It was as if, when the car left, one's own known self had gone on in it. As if one wore a new untried self to make do with, for meeting the unknown. What words one had prepared for the occasion seemed meaningless. One must simply assume that other words would come.

That day's experience was bitterly hard for some students. Some who had worked with people for many years found themselves at a loss. Papago gesture and expression were too different; they had no cue to tell them when they had begun to interest the men and women with whom they talked. Much of the time, they had to converse with the older men and women through an interpreter, through a child perhaps. Sometimes, when Papago talked with Papago interpreter, it was clear that something had interested them. But the English summary, when it came, was flat and expressionless: "He says it is hard to farm here," or, "He says he does not know."

The students had known they might fare no better. Yet each, the nutritionist and the agricultural economist and the rural sociology student, felt as if he had failed. Each

John Collier, Jr.

felt, quite irrationally, as if there must have been something in his own behavior which prevented him from establishing the satisfactory human contact he had hoped for. He came from that first day's interviews crestfallen. Indeed, the more aggressive the student's personality and the more cocksure he was that he could win friendships quickly, the more complete was his sense of flat failure. He felt that he had, after all, nothing to say to these people. He wondered, as the long afternoon dragged by, why he should try.

For all that, come evening, there was a curious content-ment among the students. Perhaps, at first, no one of them could say just what had pleased him beyond the mere ex-periencing of man's diversity. One after another, they re-ported their failures, how they'd met with blank stares of mistrust and turned backs and closed doors. But failures shared were no disgrace; and once failures were admitted, the students could tell what insights they had achieved, no matter how isolated or even apparently trivial. It was in trying to tell one another what they had seen that to-gether they began to shape what clearer questions they wanted to ask of the Papagos the next day. What one stu-dent had seen, and what half an answer another had se-cured, prompted a third to work out his own rough new concept of the terms in which Papago minds might be ap-proached. The next morning they would all start afresh—and in the month that followed, they were to walk out also among the Navahos and the Spanish-Americans of northern New Mexico. Meeting together on successive evenings, they saw how what one student had learned was springboard for another. They began to recognize how each of them had exercised his own capacities for insight. Each had projected his own background of experience, his own special inter-ests, his own self, among the peoples. What one had seen was complement and balance for the insights of another.

Together they worked out their own sensing of what it is to be a Papago or a Navaho or a Spanish-American. To-gether, too, they worked out the terms of that question their teachers had firmly refused to answer for them: "*How do I talk with a man or woman of an alien culture? How do I project myself to secure another's interest?*" They

learned which questions they could answer simply by keeping their eyes and ears open. They learned something of how they could ask the people to tell them what were better questions to ask. They reported in total a most suggestive variety of community ideas and skills and groupings and energies ready to participate in any slow, sensitive effort at growth. The pattern of a community's inaction is all too often plain to the single observer; the sensing of potentialities for action may require many observers.

What the students learned, finally, was that they could learn much about other peoples, even at the hurried pace most administrative programs impose on their personnel. At such a pace, they experienced jealousies among themselves—sometimes bitter disagreements as to the best use they could make of their little time—but they came to know that, even so, each depended on the others for perceptions and perspectives. They realized that learning is often a social process for the administrator as for the "administered." They gained an understanding of how in that social process one may become conscious, incidentally, of one's own limitations but of one's own unsuspected capacities as well.

One of the authors of the text that follows, John Adair, along with Edward H. Spicer of the University of Arizona, had field charge of this seminar in 1949, 1950, and 1951. The other author, Robert Bunker, was a student in 1949. It has been his absorbing task to read the reports of students he did not know, in the seminars that followed. The photographer, John Collier, Jr., with the seminar in 1952, tried as he said to catch the students' "instinct toward human simplicity." His selection of other photographers' work supplements his own by reflecting one strategy of the seminar: to make the physical problems and cultural diversities of Arizona and New Mexico represent those of many lands.

Though our statement of what principles we saw emerging is our own, Dr. Alexander H. Leighton—social anthropologist, physician, and psychiatrist—designed this Cornell summer seminar in cross-cultural relations. He conceived the training it would provide for administrators and technicians as a complement to another Cornell program: a study of what could be done, by administrators and technicians already trained, to anticipate change in underdeveloped nations and to help to smooth its course. We are grateful, finally, for insights he contributed as a teacher during three summers, as we are for those of Mr. Spicer and of Solon Kimball, a sociologist with rich experience in Indian administration, who joined the staff in 1952.

Part One

❧

CLASSROOM IN THE FIELD

John Collier, Jr.

Chapter 1

X

Subject: The Clash of Cultures

When, after World War II, Cornell social scientists set out to study how new technology affects ancient cultures, they naturally wanted help from the technical schools across campus. By observing the work of interested engineers, agriculturalists, and nutritionists, they hoped to learn how fear and resentment might be lessened among peoples now first experiencing rapid change. They hoped, too, to learn to teach what they learned and to demonstrate to the engineers that vast programs both must and can be administered in such a way as to gain the peoples' acceptance and support.

The time was ripe. There had arisen a more and more widespread awareness that inept human relations may not only cause the disruption of otherwise sound programs but may convert potential friends to enemies. Technology must indeed be put to work for that three-fourths of the world which, as President Truman was to put it, was without adequate food, housing, schools, or medical care. But if technology was to be free to work, technicians must be helped to evoke the peoples' desires and energies and creativity, rather than their fears. Well before the announcing of Point Four, the Carnegie Corporation granted Cornell University money for just such a "bold new program." The faculty of Sociology and Anthropology was to undertake research and training in and for the so-called "have-not" or underdeveloped areas of the world.

"The aims of the program," as then stated, were "based upon two fundamental assumptions: first, that the modern technological revolution will spread increasingly to all corners of the world; and second, that most people desire to live under conditions which offer maximum security in such basic needs as food and health. . . . It is not implied that workers in the Cornell applied social science program necessarily regard the process of modernization or westernization as in all respects a desirable one. It is felt, however, that cross-cultural studies of modern technological change may not only sharpen the tools of social science—its concepts and its methods—but may also contribute significantly to the adaptations of non-industrial peoples to the changing conditions of the modern world."

The communities studied must be chosen for their previous near-isolation from modern science. Two such were marked in Asia—a Thai village near Bangkok and an Indian village in the Ganges basin. A third was a hacienda among the Quechuas, in the heart of the Peruvian Andes. The fourth was a relocation project on the Navaho reservation in New Mexico. In all these communities but the Thai, population growth had far outstripped land resources and the peoples' primitive means for exploiting those resources. In all four, there was a desperate need for that fundamental education which is the necessary basis for economic and technological development. In all four, modern medicine was nearly or utterly unknown. These communities presented a challenge to the widest variety of engineers and educators, medical men and social scientists, to learn how the peoples could be helped to accept, with least misgivings and hurt, the sweeping material change their national leaders wanted for them.

Such study must lean heavily on what generations of scientists have discovered about culture change, about the gaining of insights in primitive societies, and about local forces facilitating or preventing change. The new stress in such study was on an inquiry into what trained administrators and technicians could do toward encouraging and building upon the forces favorable to change. The anthropologists of the study accordingly sought situations where they might know in advance what changes were to be introduced. They would be on the scene, already established among the peoples and ready to observe, rather than having to rely later on the remembered impressions of informants. By sitting in on the planning for change, they would understand both the planners' immediate and their long-term problems and purposes in detail. By working immediately with technologists, they would perceive the latter's degree of skill and success in introducing change. Through such studies they hoped to build up a body of concepts—rules of thumb about the circumstances in which change would be most likely to "take"—helpful to those governments which wish to adopt new practices but have met with local resistance.

The research itself must be of clear value to the individual engineer participating. He must learn his own capacity for imaginative work among peoples strange to his way of thinking. No set of "situational rules," for top-level planning or for blind application in the field, can insure satisfactory human relations; there must be, as well, an awakening of the social perceptions and a buttressing of the sociological experience of the engineers and administrators who will normally do the introducing of new techniques. Given such an awakening—given a series of situations in which men might study ways of establishing good relations between technicians and communities—the very rules might become more flexible. The technicians might apply today what they and their colleagues learned yesterday, in order that tomorrow they may devise and test still further possibilities for their cooperative endeavor among peoples of alien cultures.

Now it may well be objected that colleagues in settled "study areas" can achieve a degree of cooperation among themselves impossible for administrators under pressure—that engineers engaged in urgent development of resources almost never have more than a few weeks for study. Nor can they count on classroom instruction, ahead of time, in the peoples' capacity for action. It is indeed the educator's plight that he can in his classroom speak more persuasively of a world's sickness than of its capacities for recovery. Considered from a distance, a people's patterns of action can more easily be imagined as a handicap than as a potential key for development. Even the student who has never been hungry can imagine stark poverty and fear, whether or not they become for him prime, ever-present realities. He can understand the peoples' proper pride and their resentment when asked to give up what patterning or what little security they know for the sake of alien programs. He can imagine, in short, a world of monstrous forces and monstrous resistances—and himself either on the sidelines or committed to some function which he may or may not be able to fit to the demands of his fellow man. What he cannot visualize so easily is the help he may be able to get from fellow workers in fashioning his own contribution so that he may in reality serve his fellow man.

Difficulty in bridging cultural gaps is by no means a uniquely American or even a uniquely "Western" problem. Teachers in American universities have seen how the same difficulty, often in aggravated form, faces foreign students come to the United States—themselves usually the privileged few from have-not nations.

It was to meet this specific difficulty that the Cornell summer seminar in cross-cultural relations was designed. In early 1948 Dr. Leighton and Tom T. Sasaki, then a graduate student in sociology, traveled through New Mexico and Arizona seeking a community which might especially repay the proposed intensive study of change. They spoke wth agriculturalists, Indian Service administrators, local Indian leaders, and a variety of the other people of many communities. The richness of this brief field experience—the impacts of cultures briefly encountered, one after another—suggested that a similar short exposure of students to a variety of field situations might be fruitful. In particular, Dr. Leighton came to think, training through such successive impacts might show students their own responsiveness to new situations, new cultures, new sorts of human beings.

Such training would naturally have the advantages of

all field instruction; the immediacy and emotional force of personal observation should help the students comprehend the needs and desires of the peoples they went among. Representative problems and methods of solving problems were to be part of the students' own experience, more vividly than could be accomplished in any ordinary classroom. But the seminar was designed to provide another experience that can hardly be more than hinted at in the conventional classroom. Even in one short month's time the students must get the feel of their own skills and sympathies and efforts brought to bear upon such problems, in application of such methods, in truly collaborative endeavor. The seminar must demonstrate what vitality and what promise for accomplishment lie in a cross-disciplinary approach to cross-cultural problems. Which is to say, the seminar must help the students sense what are their and their world's capacities for coming to grips with their world's needs.

We have used the word *"cross-*cultural." Why not *"in-ter*cultural"? Perhaps because "intercultural" is too easily read as implying, promising, some perfectly achieved brotherhood of man; there seems conveyed in the word some idea not merely of equality of worth, but also of similarity of function on the part of representatives of the cultures involved. Let "cross-cultural" here suggest a more modest acting upon brotherhood, a working together which is the result of a literal crossing over by members of one culture to where they may help with the special concerns of the members of another (even though all may and indeed must be agreed as to ultimate purposes).

The student body—now that *was* intercultural. It was

hoped that those Asians, Africans, Europeans, Anzacs, and North and South Americans who joined the seminar would perceive one another's strengths and weaknesses. And insofar as the foreign students would be studying underprivileged areas of the United States, the seminar might become a curiously revealing Point Four in geographical reverse.

The Carnegie Corporation agreed to finance one such seminar, in the summer of 1949, as a fitting complement to the studies of change, which it was already helping to support; the Russell Sage Foundation financed three similar seminars in the summers that followed. In all, some forty students participated—five in 1949 and a dozen or so each year after. Each of the four seminars ran five weeks. Each took its students among at least three of the Southwest's peoples.

Chapter 2

Stage: The American Southwest

There seemed many reasons why the Southwest was a good stage for such a field seminar in cross-cultural relations. The whole orientation of its ancient peoples contrasts markedly with that of most of the United States, and yet the Southwest is part of the United States and easy of access. Many social scientists had had long experience among the Indians of New Mexico and Arizona; they knew individual Indians, and they knew individuals among those traders, missionaries, and administrators who work with the Indians. Reports of anthropologists going back over a seventy-year span would provide background for all the students, and reports of those geologists, geographers, nutritionists, and conservationists who have worked in the Southwest would be immediately meaningful to students with similar technical training.

Administrators' cooperation would mean access to official files and a chance for students to consult on what problems might puzzle them. Indian Service in particular could open its records of past programs, containing case histories of both dramatic successes and bitter failures in human relations. No less important, Indian Service itself was to be studied—and perhaps damned by the students before they went on to ask themselves whether such blaming was not too easy an explanation for all they saw wrong. The Spanish-Americans, in contrast to the Indians, had had access to such state and federal services as they might learn to ask for; their history could cast light on decentralization and governmental *laissez faire*.

There were striking contrasts among the peoples themselves. The Spanish-American farm communities north of Santa Fe, along the Sangre de Cristo mountains, retained some measure of their old subsistence economy, their Spanish culture, and their Catholic ritual, distinct from the ways of the Indians. And the Indians could not be lumped for consideration. The basic values, the response to Government programs, the balance struck between individual and community, all differed markedly from tribe to tribe. The students were to learn that while some cultures are easier understood than others, or seem more sympathetic, it is never simple to surmount the culture barrier. They would see that each community had some problems it was handling rather well and others which it did not seem to know how to handle at all. They would discover, in this field seminar, that adaptation is a constant process, and that they must learn to learn while going along. This Southwest was but a small working model of a world varied almost beyond belief. Studying here, the technician must be reminded of needs and aspirations all around the globe.

The paradox of man's poverty and man's mammoth

Photo Courtesy ICA

creativity, side by side, is not unique to New Mexico or

31

Photo Courtesy ICA

Arizona. There is poverty like that of the Papagos in the

32

eroded desert wastelands of Asia Minor, or where jungle

33

Standard Oil Co. (N. J.)

lands, cleared with machete and fire, furnish a bare sub-

Henri Cartier-Bresson—Magnum

sistence to the peasant farmer of South America. As in the American Southwest, water is the source of life for the herdsmen of Southwest Asia, and the dictator of agriculture

35

Photo Courtesy ICA

in India. The administrator, taking his technical aid to
men of ancient cultures, perhaps realizes that he must

Photo Courtesy ICA

achieve with them some meeting of minds. But what imagination and sympathy and broad humanity he has in him

37

for the task, he may not know. World-wide, the administrator must at times expect the peoples' blank incompre-
hension—or even reluctance and mistrust and hostility.
World-wide, he must learn to understand the "ancient's"
values, to attract the "ancient's" interest, and to shape his

program to include the "sacred cow." He must learn to

distinguish between material poverty and a people's wealth

41

of tradition, and to recognize on what dignities and joys

42

Photo Courtesy ICA

a people may build. He must learn to adapt his techniques

Photo Courtesy ICA

to the people's limited skills and resources, to increase the

Delia and Ferdinand Kuhn—Gamma

harvest while leaving it the people's own.

Chapter 3

✻

A Briefing

The seminar's first meetings, in August, 1949, were near Flagstaff, in Forest Service classrooms among tall ponderosa pines and under the San Francisco Peaks. At least one student, a cheerful Bolivian, was surprised that the seminar would soon hit the road. "And even greater was my surprise on perceiving that the students would go among the Indians for days at a time."

On another matter he expressed the shock felt by most of the students when they first observed their classmates: "There arrived the most picturesque community of students ever seen, representing six nations and four continents." The North American students alone were of many backgrounds and interests—Spanish- and Hawaiian- and Anglo-American, theorists and men of action, graduate students in anthropology and experienced overseas personnel, extension workers and specialists in labor relations or business administration. And in one or another summer, students included agriculturalists from Nepal and India

47

and Thailand and a student of economic botany from the Fiji Islands. A student of family welfare came from Egypt, and an industrial psychologist (and doctor) from Belgium. There were a Moro home economist and a nutritionist from New Zealand and a Turkish agricultural economist and a medical student from Iran.

The first lesson therein was plain: that many different nations recognize and are acting to meet their failures of production and education. A second at once followed: that their governments look to the United States for technical know-how. Their agricultural ministries look from the native hand-harvest of rice plants bearing only small beads of grain, to see how in the United States tremendous combines harvest plants heavily laden. Peruvian agronomists see how Indians of the very region where corn was first cultivated are planting much the same seed, in fields prepared by much the same foot plows, as their forefathers in Inca times—and reflect on the enormous yields North American plant geneticists are securing from recently developed hybrids. Educators in Beirut and Cairo and Athens know how few are their nations' technical schools, and how inadequately equipped, and send what students they can abroad for instruction in agriculture and mechanics. Medicine, at least as practiced in Europe and North America, has through much of the world been known only in the largest cities; since World War II, students have been sent to the United States by the hundreds for training in medicine. And they come, too, for instruction in nutrition and in conservation, and as factory supervisors and production consultants and sales managers.

Still another lesson followed. By and large seminar students from overseas knew no better than the Americans how they might address the impoverished strangers they must get to know. Nationality would not determine either crudity of approach or *savoir faire.*

Almost invariably, such young men and women from overseas are those who have had most education at home; most are from those urban areas, especially capital cities, which have had past contact with the West. Some understand foreign ways better than the lives of the rural folk of their own countries. Many exemplify how prestige is inseparably linked with the white collar over much of the world. To perform such servant's chores as are involved even in a demonstration of good nutritive practice or productive farm methods, they may think degrading. To students of good family, city-born and raised, the deep-seated, status-linked aversion to working with their hands may be something of an obstacle even during student years in America; when they return home, it is a symbol of the gulf between them and their countrymen whom they hope to aid.

Other differences between them and the rural peoples may be many and vital, lying deeper, indeed, than is easy to understand in western Europe or North America—differences in family relations and obligations, differences in economy (cash or barter), differences in faith and in ritual.

And the country folk *can* do without outside help—the farmer can still make a crop with his old plow, and the midwife can still deliver babies, and the village council can speak for the people (and the village elders can declare that vaccination is against the will of heaven). The question is what the brash innovator from the city can do.

49

Like the American technician transplanted overseas, he faces basic problems of cultural adjustment—but adjustment to his own people, in his own land. If he cannot adapt his technical knowledge to help the people make their own adaptations, there is every chance that he will not be able to function at all; for he must work within limited budgets, will probably spend much of his time chained to a desk—and cannot, like the American, simply write off a few years as one exasperating tour of duty before he gives up and goes home. M. L. Wilson, formerly Director of Extension for the United States Department of Agriculture, quotes the comment of a Cornell graduate in Lebanon on his American agricultural education: "Much of it was good, but a lot of it I can't use here at home. I was taught to measure crops, for example, with devices designed for your large mechanized farms. But here in Lebanon such units of measure are impractical; no farm produces sufficient quantities."

Year after year, in American classrooms, new foreign students show the same nearly blind faith in formal education. They look to America in the hope that through their efforts the techniques of the West, immaculate and unchanged, will spread to their native lands. Isolated as they often are from most of American life, they do not always see how these techniques have been developed for their "fit" here, and how a different "fit" in Pakistan, say, might call for a designing of other techniques.

For such students as well as for Americans who would carry their skills to foreign lands, the field seminar proposed an inquiry into the single most important concept to be added to their technical knowledge, that of the cultural whole. They must see how men's methods, beliefs, and behavior are functionally related. They must understand how new ways of living may be integrated with their people's old, interdependent ways.

Those foreign students who elected to join the field seminar were generally aware of their problem. Their consciousness of the barriers between themselves and their compatriots and of the difference in the sorts of barriers faced by the different students led to fruitful exchange of ideas before the seminar could begin. There was from the start a nervous but shared sensing of the hurdle ahead—the leap into alien cultures—and its importance.

Five days at Flagstaff gave seminar members a running start into the background they would need. They read, they asked questions, they tried their hand at stating what they wanted to look for and how they would look.

From *The Desert People,** published the year of the first seminar, the students learned about the Papagos, in Arizona and in Mexico, and their new but flourishing tribal government. Although they gain most of their cash income off-reservation, on ranches or in cotton fields or in town, the Papagos raise cattle and—like their ancestors on the same lands for two thousand years—farm with what little water is available. They are a peaceable folk, long known for their singing, their gaiety at fiesta time, and their pleasure in family relationships; their forebears took arms only with some misgivings against marauding neighbors. Although there have been many Catholic Papagos since the early eighteenth century and Presbyterian Pa-

* Alice Joseph, Rosamond B. Spicer, and Jane Chesky, *The Desert People* (Chicago, 1949).

pagos since the early twentieth, the medicine men still diagnose what transgressions have brought illness or drought, and almost all but the strictest Presbyterians take the prescribed remedial measures. Each small, tidy village is thought of as owning the land around and apportioning it by decision of all the men, meeting in council. Each village elects its own *kobanal* (from the Spanish *gobernador*) to act as mayor, sheriff, judge, and council head. The villages are interrelated by dialect groups, which until recently commanded more loyalty than "the tribe" as a whole; only in the 1930's did the Papagos begin to function as a tribe. Yet by 1949 their Tribal Council, working in close cooperation with a number of district councils, was vigorously planning and executing the desert people's own economic and social development programs.

In Clyde Kluckhohn's books and those of the Leightons,* the students read of the 70,000 and more Navahos (85,000 in the late 1950's)—by far the largest tribe in North America. They read of how Navahos migrated from country far to the north only some six hundred years ago and then, with a real genius for adapting, learned from the Pueblos to weave and to plant corn, beans, squash, and melons (as later generations learned metal work from Spanish settlers and acquired from them also horses, cattle, and sheep). They read of the elaborate Navaho rituals for curing illness, of the many matrilineal clans, and of how women usually live near their own kin and their husbands are in a sense outsiders. And the students read especially of the Navahos' recent history: of how in the 1860's "the Amer-

* See especially Clyde Kluckhohn and Dorothea Leighton, *The Navaho* (Cambridge, Massachusetts, 1946).

icans" destroyed their sheep and walked them to five years'
captivity at Fort Sumner, then back to what was now their
"reservation," and set them up in sheep again. "The Peo-

ple" scattered widely, rode and herded on some 16,000,000 acres, dwelt in their lonely cedar-log hogans, and prospered until erosion destroyed their grazing lands. After years of informal leadership by local headmen (whose authority white soldiers and administrators hopelessly overestimated), the Navahos organized their Tribal Government. By the late 1940's their Council was just beginning to grapple with new problems and new economic opportunities—but the headmen out in the communities and most of their followers were bewildered by problems, opportunities, and Tribal Government alike.

The students read of Spanish-Americans, too, especially those in New Mexico's mountain villages, so long and so remarkably isolated from "Anglo" culture.* Although since 1900 more and more men have taken wage-work away from home—in recent years, at Los Alamos—villages as remote as Truchas, in the Sangre de Cristo mountains, have retained many archaic patterns of speech and courtesy. Old, handmade furniture and farm implements still stand in sheds, where the visitor may see them if he asks, and there are still hand-spun coverings on a few floors and beds. Until recently, each village has had its leading citizen, its *patron,* responsible for helping his neighbors as they in turn have been obligated to him. Only in the 1950's have such state services as Health and Agricultural Extension work become truly familiar. And although the Presbyterian Church has many converts and a school and a clinic

* Their reading included George Sanchez, *Forgotten People: A Study of New Mexicans* (Albuquerque, 1940); Carey McWilliams, *North from Mexico: The Spanish-Speaking People of the United States* (Philadelphia, 1949); and F. Hawley and D. Senter, "Group-Designed Behavior Patterns in Two Acculturating Groups," *Southwest Journal of Anthropology,* II (1946), No. 2.

John Collier, Jr.

in Truchas, a devout Catholicism remains central to village life. The Penitentes still gather regularly for their work of brotherhood (although their re-enactments of Good Friday are less rigorous); godparents link one family to the next; and at fiesta time the wooden *Santo* comes from the church to be paraded through the streets.

The students read, that is to say, in whatever quiet moments they could find. Far more often, the instructors were at them or they at the instructors. They participated, too, in formal discussions with a variety of consultants—conservationists, administrators, anthropologists familiar with the Indian tribes and with Spanish-Americans.

In particular, the seminar staff provided data about the first people to be visited: Papago history, Papago social and political organization, the Papago way of life. Henry F. Dobyns, then a graduate student at Arizona, presented partial case histories of Indian Service introduction of technological change among the Papagos; the students puzzled out what else they needed to ask Dobyns in order to understand why one program had succeeded and another failed.

But while questioning Dobyns, the students were not always granted his articulated judgments. He borrowed a method of teaching developed by the social psychologists and called by them role-playing. He spoke briefly of Papago personality and behavior, then answered student questions as might an old Papago farmer—manner of speech, gestures, etiquette, and all. If an old Papago might not have understood a vague question or elaborate wording, Dobyns "did not understand." If a question tended to trail off or to suggest its own obvious answer, Dobyns seemed not to register that it had been asked at all. He answered such questions as were definitely put to him but volunteered no information, did not suggest what would have been a more sensible question, did not comment on the motivation of either questioner or answerer. Above all, he provided no small talk. As, one by one, the students endeavored to interview him—aware as they were that the situation was not "real"—they experienced the acute discomfort of lulls and dead ends in the talk, and tried nervously to fill in. Later they would confirm for themselves that Dobyns's "old Papago" was a truthful representation, but he was convincing enough even at the time—scrupulously polite, unhurried, unembarrassed, and apparently rather doubtful that his questioners themselves knew what they were after.

Game though it was, the role-playing served its purpose. The students experienced something of the cultural barrier that they were soon to meet and knew that their self-consciousness here in class, facing Dobyns, was very much what they would feel when they really did face a Papago. They knew that the seminar faculty would not create situations for them, but would leave them to ask themselves whether there was really anything they wanted to ask of the native peoples. They knew that they would have no time to work out the comfortably professional job of planning, each in his specialty, that "conditions" might demand. Their professional qualifications would undergo quite another testing, one designed to test their flexibility and their underlying concern for human beings: they must learn whether they could interest, and share the interests of, men and women of another culture.

In each year's seminar, some students asked for a lecture on how to interview. They were told that there is no one way to interview, that what suits one man's personality will go against another's grain, that an interview is after all a relationship between two persons and if they are to create any field of common interest they must not be hemmed all round by rules. They were, to be sure, provided with some "Don't's"—possibly with too many. But they were told to be themselves—most unsatisfactory advice to students not yet aware that such a thing is possible in altogether strange surroundings. More persuasively, perhaps, they were told that they might even burlesque themselves a bit; that if they felt inspired to some bit of nonsense, they should by all means indulge in it; that the attempt to bridge human difference can itself be a common interest. With members of one's own society, one has learned to judge reactions; one is accustomed to such cues as tone of voice, gestures, and facial expression. With members of another society, it is often necessary to improvise and exaggerate the cues, to be understood at all.

By the end of their few days in Flagstaff, the students were ready for their plunge, or "parachute jump" as they came to call it, alone among the Papagos. They were ready, that is to say, at least to watch their own reactions with some understanding. They knew they were about to experience the culture shock of finding themselves in another world—of realizing themselves in a painfully new environment. They knew, too, why they must experience it; they knew that in the final analysis culture is very largely an abstraction from patterns of human behavior and that the meeting of cultures is the meeting of each culture's least common denominators, individual men and women.

From Flagstaff, then, the students and their teachers drove directly into southern Arizona. The temperature, as they dropped down from pine country, off the plateau and across the Mogollon rim, rose steadily. By the time they reached Papago country, the desert heat was 110° in what shade was to be found. The students from the Middle East, of course, felt quite at home.

Part Two

❧

THE JUMP

Part Two

THE JUMP

Chapter 4

❧

Papagos: The Trying Out

The village Farm Manager was new to Indian country, and bitter. These Papagos just don't want to get ahead, he said. You try to help them rise out of all this. You send a schoolteacher way out here to nowhere, and half the time the parents don't care enough to make their kids attend. You work to get them a tractor, and someone lets the battery go dry.

You find out that the village here can have electricity (the Farm Manager went on) from the Project at Coolidge. You call a meeting, and you bring out a Project engineer to explain. The people come to your meeting, but not a one will sign up, not even those you know for a fact want electricity. All you can see in their faces is, "Come back in twenty years, we'll decide then."

You do get a few of them to give you some land for demonstration farming. You set them up a Farmers Association, and you negotiate a Government loan, so you can buy the equipment you need and clear the land and put

in cotton. You work, and this time the Papagos work. You're lucky, and the first year's crop nets you so much you can pay off the whole loan; your Association is clear of debts; your farmers own their new equipment; they know how cotton should be raised. But the next year they don't use the equipment; they're farming just the way they always did.

They won't spend a cent of their own on what you tell them they should have; they say they don't have the money. What gets me is, when one of them gets in trouble, in jail maybe. Boy, they can dig up fifty dollars to bail him out just like that.

Thus was the Papago "case" put before the seminar, in all sincerity, by one frustrated Indian Service employee. The question for the students, then: Are the Papagos really so apathetic? Some students, themselves with farm backgrounds, resolved to inquire whether there might be reasons other than Papago apathy for the Farm Manager's failures—Papago sense of what was practical, say, or Papago self-sufficiency. Other students would seek evidence of Papago interests and examples of Papago action.

The "case" was, indeed, far and away the simplest that the students were to encounter. They would find many elements for a tentative solution lying not too far beneath the surface.

In four days they observed the Papagos' desert environment and their desert-adapted dwellings. And in that four days each lived through the first awkward reaching out to this alien people, in their alien land:

"I started at the first house. I walked way around the house in the back before I saw anyone, and there was a very

nice-looking woman. She did not smile as I approached her where she was standing in front of her washtub out under a tree. I introduced myself and explained my mission. She did not move a muscle but stood up very close to me, looking straight at me with her black eyes. She made no reply to anything. She might have been deaf and dumb. Finally, I said, 'Well, I guess if you cannot understand English I

John Collier, Jr.

might as well go on.' She made no gesture. I have never felt so funny as I did when I walked out of that yard. I thought, What will the next be?"

But the students learned in those same four days to articulate what they had perceived, whatever the frustrations. They met with their teachers. Each student learned how others besides himself had been rebuffed. How one fellow student, hoping to eat with a Papago family, had been dismissed because "We cannot cook white man's food, we do not have a refrigerator." How another, talking for three hours with a Papago farmer, still could draw nothing but Yes and No answers.

They matched what they had seen with their teachers' knowledge. They tried to find out more precisely what questions really bore on the Papagos' situation—and what questions really interested the Papagos. Meeting thus together, they made ready to go out again alone. It was the teachers' task to help each student find himself in this new environment, to give him confidence, to help him sharpen his image of himself and his capacities when his image became blurred.

The next interviews were more successful. The students felt themselves to be more objective. They knew more exactly what they wanted to see. Where, the first time out,

John Collier, Jr.

John Collier, Jr.

they asked about "the conditions of agriculture," now they asked a farmer to show them where his flood waters came, and how he channeled them for irrigation, and where his land was washing away.

The poker face was more relaxed now. There were even

John Collier, Jr.

smiles and laughter. The farmer "told me how this flash
flood farming was pretty insecure. When crops failed, he
had lived on mesquite seeds and horse meat. But farmers
need no longer depend on flood. They have pumps for irrigation. They have good implements and good roads."

When the seminar met with Indian Service technicians, each student had his own questions to ask. The nutritionist had a question about school gardens. The medical student from Iran asked the Indian Service doctor what opportunity he had for professional shop talk. There were ques-

69

tions about conservation, about low budgets, about red tape. Indian Service was examined as closely as Papago life itself; and the students learned that by no means all Indian Servants find the Papagos "apathetic."

The students talked on into the night with some of these technicians, men of imagination and great good will and long service, who could tell of Papago progress: of the birth of the Tribal Council and its record of forceful decisions, reached after each Councilman goes back home to consult with district meetings; of Council employees and their protected tenure; of the growing effectiveness of Council committees and the development program they have drawn up;

John Collier, Jr.

of the tribe's growing self-assurance in borrowing Indian Agency help for tribal objectives.

After their four days, the students met for one last analysis of Papago problems and resources. Each threw out what ideas he thought might complement his fellows'—for his fellows' criticism. Before leaving Papago country, each must put what conclusions he had reached into report form.

What those reports indicate, again and again, is the students' debt to one another. The questions they set out to answer were those they chose themselves, but in the light of common interests. They cited one another's observations, to make their own points. They longed, some of them, for more time, so that each could bring his own sort of individual perception to subtler focus and perhaps provide himself with those growing human relationships, in this alien culture, which must underlie all true sharing. But these students, too, acknowledged that their individual perceptions must be judged in the light of others'—that among them they had evidence to show the many currents of a living society.

One student had secured a moving statement of the Papagos' love for their homeland: "This is the building where my grandmother lived. She gave it to my mother, and it is finally passed on to me. It is strong, and I will give it to my son when he marries." The New Zealand nutritionist had a hint of the Papagos' interest in other peoples, from a young Papago veteran of the war in the Pacific: "I was surprised to see the food those natives eat. I never thought I would like seaweed, but I tried it and it was good."

A Thai student and a Papago elder compared notes on a world-wide political theorem: "I said in Siam people just come and keep their mouths shut at the meeting, and go home and criticize later; my informant said that it was exactly the same thing here." A political scientist among the American students got a long account of what forms of cooperation the people take for granted. Another student reported, "When asked how they spend their non-working time, the residents of Chiuchu most commonly answered that they just sat around home. Further questioning and observation, however, revealed that that was not true"—

revealed, that is, that the people had interests and undertakings more extensive and varied than they themselves
quite realized. A Papago judge told still another student
that when the young people and the older people of his
community fell out about a livestock program, he, the
judge, did not urge their abstract cooperation, in which few
would have had faith. Rather, he "lent" each group a little
"interpretation," presumably of one another's sound objectives and over-all worth to the community. The young
people were permitted to proceed.

The nutritionist wrote of the people's pleasure in demonstrating their old ways of cooking and in preparing their
traditional foods for the interested stranger. Yet—when
challenged by a home economist—she conceded that, as else-
where all over the world, the trend toward store-bought,
packaged foods probably could not be reversed. Together
they agreed on a limited proposal for combining the best
of old and new: "Mesquite broth, prickly pear, and chollo
might be suggested to the mothers of sickly children"; for
the rest, it might be enough to urge that dried milk and
canned tomatoes be among their purchases at the store.

Among them, the students documented clearly the
Papagos' unavoidable dependence on wage-work and their
general willingness to seek it (though not, generally speaking, in mines, since from holes in the ground come evil
winds). At the same time, the students documented the
difficulties to be surmounted: the lack of schools in areas
where the Indians could find work; the insecurity an Indian might feel on his first job; his desire to keep up his
small field of alfalfa and his few cows. "I think maybe I
need money someday, maybe I'm drunk or something and

73

have no job, then I sell a cow." It was clear, too, that men absent through most of the year could not properly manage their home resources. At San Xavier, the social organization could no longer enforce fair rotation of water usage.

The picture the students came up with was of a people who accepted one change, in their eating habits perhaps, and yet feared another: "If you get electricity then you are just like the white man. . . . Bills to pay, and the bright light hurts my eyes." It was the picture of a people proud to show their old ways to the interested observer but hurt to the quick when some outsider laughed at the medicine man, a people who, once convinced that a change had to be accomplished in their manner of earning a living, wanted to make the change themselves: "When are we going to learn if we don't try?"

The students recognized, too, that here were people who, when they did try their hand at effecting a change, were generally successful. Some big stock-owners might still protest against limits on what cattle they could put on the community range: "If there are too many for the range they will die" (and the range will thus automatically be conserved). But once persuaded of the necessity, the Tribal Council administered the reduction of horses most successfully; the Agency, trying, had failed. In one district, the cattle owners, going off reservation, hired a thoroughly competent manager to run their cattle cooperatively.

The Papagos emerged as a people sometimes resentful of Government's one-sided management, for example, of the cotton-growing Farm Association. They recognized impracticalities when Government did not—for example, the uneconomic size of the individual fields and the unpre-

74

dictable supply of water where the farmers were supposed to take over Association projects run theretofore by the Agency.

Indeed, despite their poverty, the Papagos—these people among whom the students first went—had among them men of great visions. They were sharing the excitement of their first conscious accomplishments as a tribe. Many of them were by now used to the idea of change. Many looked at visitors with shrewd interest and with comparatively little mistrust (or with trust in themselves). Some now helped the students establish contact, as at least some of the students realized.

This first "parachute jump" was none the less exhilarating for being easier than another might prove. (The students' exultation was naturally the greater because they had expected failure; they reacted as to a last-minute reprieve.) Beginning here, they could appreciate both what E. B. Tylor long ago called "the psychic unity of mankind" and the peoples' real differences in behavior. As a result of their interviewing experiences, the students saw, they were more aware of their own personalities. Because of this immediate and very personal experience, each student felt himself less inclined to hide behind a professional mask. Whereas in the ordinary classroom, debating aspects of culture, students of different disciplines may fail altogether to come to terms, here in the field, studying a shared and specific problem, they gave of themselves in order to come to an understanding. The sharing of an experience under stress, and the need to communicate ideas about the shared experience, drove them together.

What they had been observing, together, was the whole

75

of a culture: the Papago. And, strikingly, they could best see what was before them only by pooling the findings of their different disciplines—that is, by studying Papago culture with every light they could bring to bear on it from their own. The meeting of culture and culture might indeed begin with the meeting of those "lowest common denominators," individual man and man. But the conceiving of over-all differences between the working principles of cultures must be accomplished in terms of those cultures considered, as nearly as possible, whole. It was the members of the seminar's teaching staff who articulated the point that there is the closest relationship between nutrition and economic level in society, and that these in turn are related to health, and that health is a dominant concern of Papago ritual. But what the teaching staff put in words, the students could accept because they had now experienced its truth. From there it was easy to go on to a further proposition: that a change in one aspect of culture very often affects the entire culture. This proposition was one most of the students had encountered before ever coming to the Southwest, but the words took on new meaning as the summary of their own experience.

Best of all, perhaps, the students knew what they had been through during the alternation of individual inquiry and group analysis. Not only did they learn together; they *observed* that their learning was accomplished by a breaking down of the barriers between their disciplines. And as they gained confidence in their ability to communicate both with native people and with one another, despite differences of language, custom, habits, or discipline, many of them very dramatically dropped one or another defense and were accepted as persons by natives and fellow students alike. Not that they had laid aside their specialized training. Rather, they wore their learning with more grace. They became more natural and easygoing—though sometimes more explosive when they did disagree fundamentally among themselves. The native peoples were quick to sense the difference and to relax in their own response. And the students found something of the Papagos (and the Navahos and the Spanish-Americans) in themselves as a result—and something of themselves in those other peoples —underlying all the complex differences in learned behavior.

Indeed, the Papago experience left some students, in a sense, overconfident. They could criticize Indian Agency personnel for this or that "blunder"; yet at the same time they could imagine themselves, as a group, manning just such an Agency. For although the seven or eight thousand Papagos and their few dozen federal civil servants faced problems big enough to be worth handling well, the scale was such that organizational relationships could remain personal. In their tiny villages, and in the district councils attended by village delegates and the Tribal Council manned from the districts, the Papagos had working units which they could understand and in which their leaders could turn directly to the problems afforded by their environment. They could watch their own progress. They could judge their Agency's progress. Federal personnel (less closely scrutinized from Washington than the personnel of larger Agencies) could tailor their assistance to real Indian needs rather than concentrate on "growing crops for the reports." And if Washington policy does sometimes change, and if Agency employees are sometimes reassigned and replaced, still among so few men and women teamwork could be achieved without elaborate "coordination." The Papagos themselves could lend much of the necessary continuity. A few imaginative administrators, briefing new employees as to *Papago* accomplishments, could provide the rest. The Papagos would automatically be brought in on the working out of federal programs because their contribution was known. Such mistakes as might be made in Papago administration, it was clear to the students, were but the honest mistakes of imperfect human beings.

It was on the Navaho visit that the students would begin to wonder whether Indian Service was not the veriest symbol of paternalism, colonialism, or even an American imperialism. Some students from countries which had known colonial rule would not judge objectively what self-government the Navahos too, and increasingly, exercise. They would see only one thing to be said: that any limits whatsoever on Navaho self-government were wrongs.

And the students would not again have the chance to imagine themselves as part of such a going concern as this they saw among the Papagos, with local partners needy but moving confidently toward their own goals. They would learn how much harder won are the interest and the trust of peoples less sure of the road ahead.

John Collier, Jr.

Chapter 5

✕

Navahos: The Challenge of Distance

The old man's hogan was many miles from his nearest neighbor's. It was the vastness of this eroded grazing land, and the Navahos' solitude upon it, that first had struck the students.

The old man touched hands with his visitors; but he clearly had misgivings. He turned to his grandson. They spoke at length in their own tongue—perhaps about where these strangers came from, or perhaps about the boy's chancing to meet them at the trading post. The strangers had asked him to interpret for them, interpret the words of another Navaho whom the boy hardly knew. He had tried, but he was uneasy; and at last the strangers had asked him whether he could not take them to someone else, someone whose words he could interpret more freely. He had brought them to his grandfather.

The old man stood silent for a long time. He did not look at his visitors. At last he sat, and the students sat around him. He answered their questions slowly and for-

81

John Collier, Jr.

mally for a while, but in the end he spoke heatedly. Especially he spoke of the Government's soil conservation policies—of how "Washingdón" had seized from him his horses and sheep and goats.

Washingdón called a meeting, the old man said. The officials who came were not any the Navahos around here knew; the Navahos around here lost their own separate reservation and did not have Agency people they knew any

John Collier, Jr.

more; there was just the one big Agency in Window Rock, for all the Navahos, and the officials came out from there. They told the Navahos they would have to reduce their livestock, that the sheep were destroying the land, eating down to the roots of the grass so that the land washed away. The officials promised that each Navaho would be paid, the old man said, paid for every one of his sheep and goats that was taken away.

Wasn't that all right, then? one student asked. If the Navahos were paid for their sheep, then they didn't lose anything, wasn't that all right?

But the old man said No. He explained that the Navahos depend on their sheep for a living. He said that mutton is their food, and that from the wool of Navaho sheep the women can make rugs. With money, he said, a Navaho can buy goods in town once; but the ewes give birth to new lambs every year. The traders know, he said; what they let a Navaho family buy depends on the size of that family's flock.

The old man answered the students' questions: How many sheep and goats and horses did he own now? How many before? Didn't he think that the erosion on Navaho lands was bad? (Yes, he did.) Wasn't it true that erosion came from overgrazing?

The grandson began to interpret. But "Doda," the old man said, "No." He knew that English word, "overgrazing." But erosion is not caused by the number of sheep the people put on their land; it is the Navaho gods who control the weather. If they send too much rain, the soil washes away; but now the gods were angry and were holding the rain back; and the grass simply could not grow. "You white men told us we would have more grass if we let you take our sheep. But look, just look around you; we have less grass now than ever."

He was willing to talk on now, unprompted. He told of how his father and mother had been prisoners of the Government at Fort Sumner eighty years before, along with thousands of other Navahos, but how when the Government let them go they were told to herd sheep. He told

John Collier, Jr.

of how the Government let them go and even gave the people sheep, and said how they should care for their sheep, and praised them when their flocks increased—until suddenly their sheep had to be taken away. "We don't trust Washingdón any more, those white men there can't make up their minds."

Among the Navahos it was distance that the students

John Collier, Jr.

struggled to realize—the distance between Navaho neighbors, the distance between Government and governed, the distance sometimes between questioner and answerer. Or the distance between the wage-earner, gone to work on the railroad or in the carrot fields, and his family left at home. "The man spends his money in town. And sometimes the woman runs around at home, she doesn't take care of her children."

The miles of reservation roads, as the students learned firsthand, were a formidable barrier. And some Navahos in the past had wanted them so. They had dynamited water tanks built for their benefit, and filled wells with fine sand, lest the land be so green as to tempt white Americans to seize it.

There was the immensity of time to be sensed, too. Women work for the five cents an hour their weaving may bring. And men plant their corn as did their ancestors long ago, in clusters. (The agronomist from Nepal at first thought such planting "faulty." But he reported soon that the method was proper after all, in such a land, to conserve moisture and to insure some harvest where cutworms abounded.)

John Collier, Jr.

John Collier, Jr.

John Collier, Jr.

From Indian traders, the students learned how the Navahos try to live through their seasons of direst need—by
pawning their beautifully wrought silver and turquoise.

They asked Navahos what credit they could expect at the
traders'. And once convinced that their questioners were
honestly interested, these Navahos spoke at length, not
only of how the traders will always furnish bare necessi-

John Collier, Jr.

ties, but also of the people's overwhelming material poverty and need for cash employment now, no matter how
hard the first adjustments might be.

A Hindu student heard from missionaries that the Nava-

John Collier, Jr.

hos must give up their old ways. A young Navaho boy these missionaries had adopted talked of the life he hoped to lead.

But a medicine man told a Belgian doctor that there

John Collier, Jr.

need be no conflict between white values and Navaho—that the doctor might know how to pull out his wife's teeth, but could not cure his daughter's bad dreams. "They want me to throw medicine away, I cannot. Some things white doctors do not know how to cure, but we know, we have medicine."

Space and the quiet flow of time, immediate problems

and the Navahos' own sense of a century's misunderstandings—all were on a vast scale. And the students sensed in some Navahos an unlimited composure. The old man who gave his afternoon to explaining the techniques of desert farming later accepted gifts of food in such a way as to make clear what high ethical value the Navahos set on generosity.

The old-time Indian policeman, asked about Government programs, gave answers he knew other white men had liked, until persuaded that the students were truly interested in his individual opinion. Some Navahos were painfully shy on first meeting; many younger women put hands or even shawls over their faces, and giggled. In crowds, when individual student and individual Navaho had not explored common interests, the students met only Navaho silence. But when a Navaho knew some purpose for speaking, he spoke earnestly and, often, eloquently. When, at a Navaho wedding, one student from Asia spoke briefly of his country and his family and his work, the Navahos clustering around were moved to respond. Their interpreter touched the student's head lightly and told him, "They say you must be a leader in your country, your hair is gray and you have wisdom. We are glad you have come this long way to our land and we wish you could stay."

And indeed the students were not embarrassed by Navaho silences as they had been among the Papagos. They learned that they could wait for clear cues to Navaho reaction, that even in their few short days they could make contact if they did not force the pace. What little they had been taught about Navaho etiquette—not to ask a person's

John Collier, Jr.

name, not to look a person in the eye—was enough somehow to put them at their ease till they could sense for themselves the Navahos' real courtesy. With even so much sure-

ness of their welcome, the students had time to learn how to ask questions that might evoke Navaho response. In particular, they learned that although their young interpreters could rarely handle generalizations, by means of precise and specific questions they could create with older Navahos some shared understanding of purpose. The Hawaiian student learned how many new crops and techniques the "conservative" Navaho farmer *had* adopted over the decades. An American home demonstration agent found Navaho women eager to sew using new patterns, once she showed them that they did not really need brown wrapping paper, but could use newspaper or whatever was to hand. An Egyptian girl learned how Navahos' refusal to go on planting a new hybrid corn—a refusal quite baffling to male civil servants—had sprung from Navaho women's dissatisfaction with the new corn flour and meal. Together the students learned what community interest they could arouse and what added insights they could, among them, achieve by working with what material was to hand and in response to specific community demand.

From their instructors, the students learned that the Navahos' acceptance of and demand for "white man's" schooling and medicine had come about dramatically in the last fifteen years. Again from their instructors, the students learned that within the past four or five years the Navaho Tribal Council had, with Indian Service advice and encouragement, moved from the status of puppet government to impressive and independent management of many tribal affairs.

But what the students experienced for themselves was that, as yet, few Navahos knew where federal regulations left off and where, accordingly, their tribal action began and their own individual action could surely begin. Again and again the students found the Navahos recounting battles lost fifteen years before: stock reduction, and the consolidation of six smaller Navaho reservations into one vast domain. It was clear enough that both battles had been conducted by federal personnel with an almost total disregard for Navaho understanding and Navaho willingness to assume responsibility. Consolidation and rule from Washington had disrupted, not only the old personal relations between the Navahos and their local "Agents," but the Navahos' local chapter organizations as well; the new Tribal Council had drained off local leadership before the people had any chance to see that the interests of all the Navahos were in many respects, and increasingly, one. When that new Tribal Council was asked to rubber-stamp stock reduction, with an eye to maximum tribal income in the long run, the people in their isolated communities could feel only that "Washingdón" was manipulating their lives capriciously. The individual family was in most instances left with so small a flock that the natural increase was not enough to feed the family—let alone feed those poorer relatives to whom a Navaho has deep-felt obligations.

As one country-bred American student wryly put it, "If the Navahos place a value on having lots of sheep so that they may slaughter them for social gatherings, a program designed to reduce the number and improve the quality of the sheep is destined to opposition." And the Hawaiian student reported that the hybrid sheep the Navahos were urged to introduce and sell at higher prices were such as the Navahos knew could not survive long droughts. The year-by-year result, as a Canadian observed, was that small stock-owners ate their remaining sheep and cows while the number of their goats and horses steadily increased. Consequently—a Hindu concluded—there was a breakdown even in family life. There was an abrupt stop to that conscious and deliberate education of children to responsibility which Navaho parents had traditionally accomplished by giving the children their own livestock to care for. "Poor families used to go to their neighbors for flour or corn to tide them over," a Navaho woman said, "but none of this goes on now. At the time of the reduction the small owners felt they were being hit hardest, and the big owners began to be jealous of their neighbors on relief."

Sometimes, to be sure, the students could not determine whether the federal programs criticized were those of the past or the present. The central failure that had clearly continued into the present, was the failure of communications. Navahos spoke of successive grazing regulations as "the blue paper" and "the white paper," with no idea of what change in regulations the change in "papers" had effected. The community leader whom Agency officials thought to be an enthusiastic supporter of the new regulations, proved in conversation with the students to understand those regulations almost not at all. On a relocation project, Navaho farmers could understand neither how water was to be shared for irrigating nor what right they had to keep the lands they might improve. "I can't figure these Navvies out," a farm agent said; "a lot of them would rather work for a white farmer, for pay, than grow their own crops on their land." But, "It's not my land, you know," one Navaho farmer explained to a student from the seminar. The farmer had been chosen by the Government for a demonstration of the worth of manure. He sat with the student on his fence, watching Government trucks dump the manure and a Government spreader level it out. He talked of how perhaps if he could understand the regulations he would know whether he could keep this land, and his son after him; but how they could never be sure they might not do something wrong, and forfeit their claim.

"It sure is nice of the Government to fix it up this way," he went on, "but I don't know where we could get any more manure, for the neighbors' fields. All the corrals have been cleaned out."

Other farmers told how, when they bought the cooperative machinery the Government urged on them, there might be no one with authority to make sure it was repaired. Or how, after they had worked to pay for "community" machinery, the Government could add new members to their association, who neither had helped buy the machinery nor knew how to use it with care.

In the fine, new day schools, too, the students learned how impractical the Navahos thought "Washingdón." The battered old boarding schools, a medicine man said, had taught young Navahos more intensively what white ways they must know:

"Schools are no good any more. Teachers do not teach, they clean their buildings. We want our children in school all day, to learn English."

The student from India summed up what divergent goals might attract the educators and that Navaho parent most earnestly concerned with his child's education for the

modern world. Such a parent, he reported, "does not want Navaho teachers to be employed in schools, since he considers that children learn English quicker from white teachers. He prefers Government schools to mission schools, since the latter spend much time in religious instruction. He prefers residential schools, to teach English quicker and incidentally provide good food at no cost. There is an identity of interests and immediate objectives between the Government and the people. And yet there is a gulf between their ultimate objectives." The Navahos "want to hold tenaciously to their culture while using education as a means of making a better living." But educators hope to teach in terms of over-all values, both Navaho and non-Indian.

Meeting once again in seminar, the students learned how very many instances they had collected of sheer breakdown in communications between Indians and Indian Service. Some students had reacted emotionally, against Indian Service or more generally against what they considered American colonialism, but for the most part they avoided mere blaming as they avoided all pat solutions. It is indeed evidence of the value they put on their own approach to the problem as a group, that their stress was not baldly on the need for communications between groups (between Indians and Indian Service) but equally and perhaps even primarily on the need for communications within each group (among the Indians, and among Indian Servants). Given such "lateral communication" among men of good will, the students seemed to feel, enough resourcefulness would be brought to bear so that what communication was achieved between groups could be expanded, appreciated, and built upon.

The students urged that even in those areas where some Government projects had been most crudely sabotaged, other projects had been successful when Navaho public opinion had been given a chance to form. They urged that some Indian Service experiments in helping the Navahos create their own forums had at least shown how much more could be done; they cited the Navaho newspaper and Navaho broadcasts on a local radio station and the way the

Tribal Council was at last being allowed to make its own mistakes. But they urged at the same time that such experiments would prove little unless Indian Service technicians learned to communicate with one another, so that one could learn what results another had achieved and so that they could make use of one another's momentum. And they remarked that if they themselves were a community, eager to exchange ideas, they were so by virtue of having been set to inquiring together.

They urged, above all, that "lateral communication" could flourish among the Navahos, or for that matter in the Indian Service, only when there was something to communicate. The point was made by a student with Information Office experience in Japan: "The medium will develop when it has matter to carry. If Tribal Council meetings and possibly Council committee hearings could be broadcast, and if news, opinion, and sustaining programs could be developed, it may be the radio will soon come into its own."

A nutritionist commented that what she had to teach might be most important for the channels it might open—as a start toward women's learning together and working together. "Several women suggested that some instruction in home management would be welcome, for it would provide a subject of common interest not associated with previous disturbances. Every effort should be made to pass on information to these people in such form that it is possible for them, in turn, to practice it *in the community*." Whereas "planning provides an opportunity for the technician and the people to work together, it is "the working out of the program" which may "cause social ties within the community to be strengthened." "It is encouraging," another student wrote, "that some chapter members feel dissatisfied with the inadequate reporting they get of Tribal Council plans."

It was clearly not only or even primarily Navaho traditional institutions which the students felt might be "utilized." Rather, they were concerned that whatever the groupings in which men and women seemed ready to act or discuss, they be helped to find stimulating agenda. If the Navahos want more English and less plumbing in "their" schools, let them have their way; let their education develop its own momentum; interest in better schooling "will increase," the Hindu student insisted, with an increase "in the efficiency of their businesses, in their political activity, in Navaho utilization of leisure, and in the bettering of their conditions of living generally."

So, too, with those engineering and agricultural divisions of Indian Service in which Navahos can gain practical know-how. The chance for technical experience was found invaluable. But the Navahos who sought it should be helped to find ways to work ever more closely with their fellow tribesmen; they were in fact cut off again and again from any such cooperation. The Belgian student found Navahos in Indian Service were regarded as "Quislings, less accepted than whites," because they so often had to follow instructions literally and could not adopt the suggestions of their neighbors. They should, rather, be brought into construction programs so flexible as to invite local discussion. As the Hawaiian student put it, an Indian Service engineer will ordinarily build, of steel, the "strong and beautiful bridges which require the most skilful technicians. But if we judge his achievement by the number of Indians he has succeeded in training to build bridges of durable but of local products, logs, he will have many Indians employed."

One seminar member drew from an Indian Service engineer the suggestion that, perhaps, "if you are going to settle people on a project you had better get a balanced cross section which has the capabilities and units for the traditional organizational systems." It was not a static society that that engineer proposed. He, and the students, had come to think in terms of the careful matching of community members' skills with the tasks before them. In particular, the students were articulating their belief that members of a community faced with problems they *can* handle *will* handle them and, in the handling, will learn from one another how they may tackle yet other problems. Incidentally, what they gain from one another will probably include what some of them have learned from "the outside."

The students came away from the Navaho with no confidence in any one set of "answers," either for reservation management or on how to sell a program to Navahos. Rather, they had learned from Navahos and from various observers alike what more general communication is possible, rewarding, necessary as context for almost any sort of local program, and yet sometimes desperately hard to achieve. They had seen that such communication is not in any sense automatic or natural or dependent merely on good will—that it must be thought through and arranged for, and that its breakdown does not necessarily stem from hatefulness or excessive stupidity. They had observed what barriers to understanding may exist without quite destroying men's desires and capacities to break through them. They had realized that any one man, any few men, may start or end up with blind spots. They had found that in so harsh a situation as the Navahos', many may despair of accomplishment, despair even that there may come to them new insights worth analysis, new ideas worth acting on.

Suppose, that is to say, that by some accident some of these very students should be assigned to work with the Navahos. They must themselves anticipate frustrations and misunderstandings. They must expect sometimes to run out of insights and ideas in their search for how advances in technology might be harnessed with Navaho concepts of right community decision and right individual responsibility. But they knew now for themselves that such insights and ideas existed among the Navahos as they did, presumably, among other peoples, regardless of misunderstandings. They had seen that the joint canvassing of such insights and ideas may lead to new mutual understanding and still further grasping of possibilities for action. They did not see any end to the Navahos' road—either a dead end or some "arrival." In their own future assignments, they would, they hoped, be the less hasty.

John Collier, Jr.

John Collier, Jr.

Chapter 6

✕

Spanish-Americans: Family Album

What the students knew in advance about the mountain villagers of New Mexico had to do especially with families and fears. They knew something of how community pressures, working on the heads of families to direct even their grown children aright, still largely determines economic and social activity. And they knew what mistrust most Spanish-Americans still feel toward the outsider who taxes their lands or pries into their penitential observance of Good Friday. The students were to learn almost nothing about the people's faith or about the self-scourging Penitentes. About families and the land, the students would learn so much as to amount to their own original research contribution. They would be slow expressing what rub of personal relationships they observed; some would fall into facile defenses of this or that new or old economic interest. (In Truchas, far more than in the less familiar Indian communities, the students would feel and must reckon with antagonisms among themselves as part of "the situation" in which men must work.)

But what—once more as a group—most students would see at the end of their short stay in Truchas was a village life in which every faction had its important part to play. Moving slowly from subsistence farming to wage-work, the people must expect some conflict in values. They must recognize that neighbors will disagree as to which value should be held most dear, or as to how the conflicting values can best be reconciled. Each student would find just what his fellows found in the way of grumbling and apparent resentment directed by the villagers against one another. Signs of enduring ties among the villagers were less immediately obvious: the students must compare notes to discover, in sum, what deep fondness the villagers shared, fondness for each other and for their home.

Community quarrels here seemed like family quarrels. The old man who railed against the young wage-workers' failure to keep up their fields admitted when pressed that he was scolding to no purpose, that only a major depression could really send them back to subsistence farming. Many villagers told the students how all the extra cash went into drink; but if asked, they were just as eager to tell how the new cash went into furnishing and repairing houses. They might tell of petty self-seeking and the breakdown of village cooperation, now that more and more men worked for wages; but they might add how, when a little *more* wage-work became available—when the wage-workers could begin to think a little beyond each week's paycheck—there was less temptation to be petty, and new forms of cooperation began to emerge.

No villager, it seems, went so far as to claim absolutely that the people could solve new problems while retaining old prides. But the Bolivian student, despite some firsthand knowledge of community breakdowns, was willing to make such a judgment himself. Weighing what variety of impressions his fellow students reported—and with no language barrier to his own communication with the villagers —he concluded that "the gradual incorporation of the minority people into the nation" was being accomplished in Truchas by "the reconciling of local traditions and new modes."

Some students found reasonably informative acquaintances over beers in a bar. Some talked in the street with a village dissident, eager to tell all—and for the first time were sure they disliked a "native," even after they were reasonably sure they understood him. Some watched Truchas's constant friendly wrestling matches until villagers started casual conversation.

The Hawaiian student found himself the star of an evening at the Presbyterian mission, showing his colored slides of home and demonstrating the missionary ladies' new projector before an inquisitive and enthusiastic audience. The Siamese student compared dance steps with an old man of the village, before another crowd.

Those students came quickest to an understanding of village workings who went into homes. Some four younger male students failed in Truchas one summer, standing aloof, huddling together. They hesitated to give of themselves, or they had no personal experiences they could contribute to family conversation, or perhaps Truchas simply assumes that such young men could have nothing to contribute. But students over twenty-five could swap views on change as they themselves had experienced it, and in pass-

John Collier, Jr.

ing they could shake their heads at the irresponsibility of the young. And the girls could always help wash dishes, so naturally that they reported "no embarrassment" on either side. One girl became "her" family's unofficial "niece," and her picture was taken—alone, please—for the family friend, away in Wisconsin, who would surely want to marry her.

The students learned, at late family suppers, of their hosts' long hours of wage-work at Los Alamos and of their slow rise to better-paid jobs there.

John Collier, Jr.

An older man told them of the ingenuity necessary for successful farming in the old days, and of how he had made his own mill and his own threshing machine.

The students learned, at "their" family's store, how hard it is for the individual farmer to find any market where he can profitably sell his crops.

Over the weekend, when his host was home by daylight, the agronomist from India learned how to use a New Mexican plow, and how to make do with little water.

Like other students, he found the family with whom he lived eager for news of the outside world. He told of his people's crops and land. He told how his own family in India keeps house: "Once a week we spread the floors with cow manure." His audience was captivated.

Indeed, it was as the students showed their own sympathy with the joys and problems of family relationships,

John Collier, Jr.

that the balances and mechanics of village relationships
were explained to them. They heard little jealousy expressed of any family head's success in finding good work;
but if a man let his young sons and daughters work at Los
Alamos, his neighbors might lament that, with cash in their
pockets, the sons and daughters would escape family control. The students observed how an Anglo woman, mar-

ried to a villager, had many friends; if anyone in the community still resented her, she did not seem to know it; but her husband increasingly feared such resentment and had almost decided to move away.

The well-to-do Catholic villager who was something of a *patron* and the devout Presbyterian who was handyman at the mission, though at odds on other issues, alike urged

John Collier, Jr.

on the students that any cooperative venture, to be successful, must be so planned as to ask something of the participating families that each could afford to give. The students witnessed for themselves this pride of sharing. Among
immediate neighbors, there was pride that one could still
help till the sick friend's fields or help build the neighbor's new house. Of one rich man's wife who persisted in

doing all her own housework, it was not said merely, "She is too mean," or "too stingy," but, "She will not let us help."

Living as they did with families, the students learned how conscious the people were of change in their lives— not as something to be for or against once and for all, but as an unending series of decisions and experiments. Many houses and the Catholic church as well were hard-plastered now; most men could no longer find time to re-plaster every year with adobe, and some thought that the hard plaster looked better. Most families had replaced the wooden chairs round the walls of their living rooms with new overstuffed armchairs and sofas. Some—not knowing, perhaps, whether their visitors would praise or blame—explained the store-purchased rugs on their floors with the statement that women nowadays had not the time to weave the old strip carpets. Most had new refrigerators, and alongside the cold pop there might be vegetables, for if few men raised their own now, some bought fresh produce on their way home. Almost all the women still cooked on wood stoves; come Saturday and Sunday, a man enjoyed the trip into the mountain forests for free fuel.

The building of a dam, not many years back, had become such a political issue that at last it fell through. Even now, in private conversation, few villagers were wholly sure whether or not the dam would have benefited them. Surely they needed water. Yet even for water, to mortgage their land, as they would have had to do, was to court disaster. It might be that the few well-to-do farmers who argued against the dam were merely selfish, for they had more water already than most. At the same time, there was undoubted truth in those farmers' arguments. It was true that the Government would make all the village pay for what would mostly help the west side. And it was true that many farmers in a village nearby had not been able to pay assessments after their dam was built, and had lost their land. One agronomist among the students hunted up federal officials for their explanation of such failures and learned that there had indeed in the past been "inadequate planning, inadequate education, and assessment laws written into contracts but never explained, so that there was taxation without previous knowledge." Very likely—as well as the students could judge—there was nothing in the proposals now put to Truchas that the people did not know about in advance; but like the Navaho sitting on the fence, they could not be sure. In contrast, when the villagers were asked to help build a clinic at the Presbyterian mission— not to sign papers, but to come work—all but two families did help. In fact, too many wanted to help; those who could not be useful in the building of the clinic set to work instead, Presbyterian and Catholic alike, on new quarters for the Presbyterian missionaries.

The students, when they met together to discuss what they had learned in Truchas, found that they must first thrash out what were the right questions to be asked. There were some who wanted to blame Government bungling, or the richest villager's selfishness, or all the villagers' timidity, for anything that did not go exactly right in Truchas. There was, indeed, much to be said in blame. Government agencies, federal, state, and county, were often hopelessly uncoordinated in their effort to work with the people. Perhaps the one most conspicuously well-to-do

farmer and trader did want the full old-time influence of the *patron*, or did fight some innovation simply because he could not imagine democratic accomplishment. And apparently some villagers have refused to learn English because they do not want their children correcting their pronunciation; apparently some villagers have refused to live where they could find better jobs, through fear of ridicule.

But about the levels of government it should be said as

well—the students pointed out—that any full, meaningful coordination must be achieved in terms of what the *villagers* may find they want to secure among new values, and protect among old.

Similarly, it should be said of those villagers who fear to move, that they do sometimes encounter ridicule and racial animosity and prejudice. One student might know more than the others of how the Texans recently moved into the area were scornful of "Mexicans" or "greasers." Looking at the problem together, however, all the students could agree that any fear of discrimination or failure was only one force binding the people of Truchas to their community. They stayed or came back because of strong bonds of attachment to their kinsmen, to their mountain independence, and to their whole way of life.

The richer villagers might sometimes work against specific proposals—against "progress"—but their influence was at most inconclusive. Their neighbors' criticism of them was often naive—for example, that the storekeeper expected to make a profit not only on cash transactions, but when his customers paid him in kind. In any event, the people were not at his mercy. Most families had trucks now and could buy and sell in the big towns of the valley. One student learned that many families had cleared off their debts at the store; and other students, talking with the storekeeper himself, concluded that he understood very well how his business now depended on his keeping his prices competitive.

Naturally, the students asked themselves whether the people of Truchas might not find more ways to work together if they were still, like their grandfathers, all of one

John Collier, Jr.

religion. In a neighboring village, there was evidence of real religious bitterness. Catholic teachers were believed to grade Protestant schoolchildren unfairly, and a Protestant woman was said to have taken photographs of the Penitentes' meetings, just for spite. But in Truchas—though Presbyterians were likely to be Democrats and wage-workers, while most Catholics were Republicans and subsistence farmers—the split did not seem deep. For the women of the Presbyterian mission centered their activities around what the people recognized as their great needs, in the classroom and in the clinic; they seemed more concerned with service than with conversion. They taught Catholic children as well as Protestant. They gained the people's cooperation where outsiders, coming in only long enough to sell projects to some few "leaders" or "progressive farmers," necessarily failed.

John Collier, Jr.

The students, talking together, did not minimize the problems they saw facing the Spanish-Americans of New Mexico's mountain villages. They saw that new troubles would arise and old methods break down. Truchas's irrigators already had more and more trouble finding a mayordomo to supervise their sharing of water for the trifling pay they could afford to give him. Sometime soon the wageworkers must conclude that their weekend farming was never going to pay off. Either they must concentrate on small kitchen gardens, or they must join in hiring the help they needed for economical tilling of the soil and marketing of crops. Once they were sure enough that wage-work would continue and that they would not have to fall back on what little they could grow, they might start pondering how they could best gain an income from their land without loss of the feeling, family by family, that as the land had been their fathers' so would it be their sons'.

The students had not, any more than among the Papagos and the Navahos, learned to determine definitively what should be done for the people. What they had learned was how they could come to know the people's aspirations and energies. And to know these, they saw, was to want to work alongside and to share in the search (as the Bolivian student put it) for "new types of values with elements of both cultures, and without conflict."

Part Three

❧

THE SEARCH FOR MEANINGS

Milton Snow—Navajo Service

Chapter 7

❧

The Students Summarize

One year's seminar took a quick look in at the Colorado River Reservation, with its sometimes bitter division between the long-time residents and some Navahos only recently "resettled." Once students visited a Hopi Pueblo during late July's dances. Though they won some special fame as "visitors who sleep on the roof," they were for the most part regarded simply as tourists, whose friendly interest might be rewarded with casual talk. Some students spent at least a few hours in one or another New Mexico Pueblo, and these complex, tight-knit communities gave them new perspectives, revealed new contrasts between peoples.

But Papago, Navaho, Truchas—by and large, those were the course. The students had lived now among the peoples of those three societies, two Indian and one derived from sixteenth-century Europe. In each they had subjected themselves to the tension of making one's identity known to a stranger and coming to realize the stranger's own essential quality as well. They had recorded separate impressions of each society visited. Now, as a final task, they must put on paper what they thought they had learned about human encounter.

They wrote of specific perceptions. They wrote of techniques they had tried. They wrote of how sometimes when the techniques failed, people and observer might understand one another the better simply because they had watched one another during the failure. Above all, they wrote of encounter itself as something real—not just as politically urgent, not even just as psychologically unnerving though sometimes warming (or warming though sometimes unnerving), but as a challenge fascinating for its own sake.

This challenge was reflected in the students' very choice of peoples to write about in their final summaries. They wrote comparatively little of Papago country, for they had found little lasting difficulty of communication there, at least on the level of inquiry they had explored, a whole month ago, in their first "jump." They wrote extensively of Navaho problems, largely because they could not imagine that these could ever find any quick or easy solution. They wrote of how Spanish-Americans may be helped to adapt their traditional cooperative ways to new undertakings. And then they wrote about the Pueblos. They had seen the pride that is in the faces of the men and women of Hopi or Tesuque or Santo Domingo; they had climbed to Hopi villages or walked into the comfortable homes of the New Mexico Pueblos; but they had only barely begun to understand these people.

They could have claimed successes in their brief interviews with Pueblos. But by now they were not impressed

John Adair

John Adair

with what friendly but superficial responses they might gain from a people clearly more accustomed than most Southwest Indians to casual passers-by. By now, they were not complacent about being allowed to hear the set speech on "Problems" of a leader who an Indian Service school teacher said wouldn't talk to her at all. By now, they could

John Adair

resist the temptation to believe that if people "speak English," then communication has necessarily been achieved, and they reflected on how an interpreter may facilitate the flow of ideas as well as words. They had talked with Pueblo Indians only long enough to perceive what reserve and sometimes, they felt, what despair may lie beneath the ami-

131

able chatter. Yet in his final paper many a student set down especially what clues suggested a tentative approach to the Pueblos, had he time to live among them.

The students were dog-tired from the effort they had put into the understanding of alien peoples. In the few hours allowed them for their reports, they could not possibly express and qualify each idea, each observation, precisely. Given a month for their reports, they would probably have bogged down in a hopeless effort at marshaling facts and impressions. Given one day, they knew they must confine themselves to what they felt most strongly, what they felt really impelled to record.

Each student worked from notes he had compiled in the field. These were the details of personal experience from which he must abstract general principles. He had had to learn rapidly; now he might, like his instructors, reflect that one reason he had learned so much was the very stress he had been under.

That some students had naturally learned far less than others was evident from their reports. Some few, indeed, did not seem to have been touched personally; they had confused their efforts with those of a formal research team, and they left the seminar with no sign of new idea or outlook. But others wrote extraordinary reports. They knew suddenly that they had something to say; one had been moved to strong expression by the Navahos' situation and another by close sympathy with the people of Truchas. Though what they had learned was so complex in its personal connotations that not all could be put on paper, most of the students did find words for their new perceptions. They knew they had learned something of how to use the anthropologists' special information about cultures when it was available, and how to make do without it when it was not. They knew they had learned to survive the first awkwardness in an unfamiliar community, and that a very little knowledge of that community's etiquette would ease the awkwardness enormously. They knew they had learned to trust their own stock of human sympathy and imagination. Their growth made fine reading.

The reports were supposed to be in the form of a letter—a letter written to a friend going out to Africa, say, or Southeast Asia, for some program of technical and economic aid. The imagined friend had never worked among peoples of any culture but his own. What advice could the student give his friend? What could the student tell him about cultural barriers and about human understanding?

In their reports the students tried to express what rules they felt were basic for cross-cultural undertakings. Many of their "rules," naturally, were like those taught in conventional classrooms. But they were also the direct expression of what the students had seen for themselves. "Programs must be developed through the existing social organization"—as the Papago Tribal Council had its roots in traditional village groupings and as the Navaho Council did not. "There must be good lateral communications among the staff before programming is attempted"—the principle harked back to the whole body of relationships, good, bad, or achingly inadequate, which the students had seen within Indian Service and among the civil servants who work with Spanish-Americans.

"Don't begin to seek data from someone you meet for the first time. Don't seek your data until you have found something of yourself in this person whom you meet, and something of him in yourself." The words are those of an especially articulate and experienced student; the underlying idea appears in the narrative of student after student reflecting on first meetings.

"Ask yourself, 'Whose program is it?' Do the people in the community feel that it is theirs or merely yours?" It was the students' pledge to themselves that they would remember to ask themselves such questions.

They were quick to report their own boners. One student told how he had made the mistake of interviewing an old man in a Pueblo in the same way he had talked with other peoples less accustomed to outsiders. ("One should use much more direct questions, go to the point at once. . . . They are too 'white' not to catch the meaning of the indirect. They laugh at you when your question is too childish.") He had wanted to know what the old man thought of changing values and had therefore "skilfully" asked, "If you were a girl, whom should you like to marry? A farmer, a worker at Los Alamos, or a teacher?"

"I don't know," the old man said. "I am not a girl." When asked directly, he explained in detail what changes in values he had observed.

The same student listened while a visitor from Washington asked a young Santa Clara woman what her family ate. The young woman answered, "American food."

The visitor took out notebook and pencil and asked, "Please tell me, what do you have for breakfast, lunch, and dinner?"

The young woman hesitated, then turned and spoke in

Tewa to her mother across the room. The student observer reflected how in his own land a proud member of a minority people might want to answer, "We eat as well as you—no corn meal or stew for us." And such was the answer he reported:

"She related thus:

'Breakfast: ham and eggs or bacon and eggs, cereal, milk, coffee.

Lunch: fried potatoes, cold meat, bread, and milk.

Dinner: roast beef, vegetables, salad, bread, and milk.'

She said no more. The interview ended."

The students had sensed bitterness among some of the Pueblos, especially those who held regular jobs like their non-Indian neighbors. Their specific complaints were not always realistic. An Indian whose sons had as good jobs at Los Alamos as anyone else without special training, nevertheless insisted that "all whites" there "don't know anything" but nevertheless "start at the top."

Another either mistook his history or spoke, un-Pueblo-like, for other tribes than his own, when he told some students, "A long time ago the Anglo took our land and killed our people."

But the bitterness expressed itself especially in conflict within the Pueblo, the students reported. There were "much drinking and disorder," "a schism between the elders of the village and the young," "resistance against programs designed for the communal welfare." As one student explained,

"If an Indian Service administrator looked into the current history of this Pueblo he would find relatively well-to-do wage-workers causing friction by their newly acquired independence in a village that has been completely communal in the past. . . . The old religious organizations, the ritual dances and kiva activities, confuse rather than orient the participants in the face of the contradictory dogmas of Christian sects."

And again:

"When a man becomes more acculturated, he is even more sensitive to all that tends to keep him out of the group he fought so hard to belong to. Leaving one god to pray to another is already a hard job without having to bear the burden of being rejected by that god. It was with great emotion that this young woman spoke about the discrimination manifested in Los Alamos towards the Indians."

The students had debated what blame they could put on Indian Service. Heads of Agency divisions they did not judge too shrewdly, for, interviewing these in offices, they tended to accept as the whole truth one official's articulation of a liberal philosophy (worded precisely as at the start of his career) or another's show-me reaction to proposed new programs. Observing in the field, the students naturally saw more clearly into the civil servant's blend of horse sense and imperceptiveness. A farm agent stopped his car by a field where a young Indian was busy plowing.

"Come over here," he called.

"What for?" the Indian returned, and went on with his work.

Yet the same agent seems to have persuaded the leaders of Santo Domingo Pueblo to round up and sell the useless horses on their range by showing them they could thus afford to buy the sprayer and insecticide they wanted.

In the end, the students blamed Indian Service only as one factor among many—blamed its employees only for not possessing more than average humanity. Those older Indians, for instance, who had first tried to show their people new economic opportunities, often needed extraordinary help in their own confusion between Indian and non-Indian ways. One such, who talked with the Hawaiian and the Belgian student, "did not agree with the industrialization of his country, but was eager to see his son get a job in Los Alamos. He criticized the way Indians handled the community hay machine, but was doing it more harm than anyone else could. He was bitter to the whites, but had two sons-in-law who were whites and was proud of them. He felt rejected by his people and the Indian Service and could find no other way to save his ego than by rejecting them."

The students had had their good moments in the Pueblos. The Hawaiian, declaring himself a Hopi, could not then persuade his hearers that he had only been joking: "We are of the same blood," he was told firmly. One student found a "stern patriarch" surprisingly willing to talk, "apparently aware that no harm would come" from discussing community problems with an earnest stranger. Three girls—Egyptian, Moro, and American—reported the "warmth" of first meetings with Pueblo women and their own "ready entry" into spacious, well-to-do Pueblo homes. But whereas "Navahos, less receptive on initial meeting, after short contact often poured out some of their troubles," the same students found that here they could not "go beyond the superficial or broach subjects of more intimate concern." They came to see that an administrator among the Pueblos must settle for slower responses and, above all, must work in terms of *community* response and adaptation: "Every change will affect the whole structure and will be very difficult to realize."

The students naturally contrasted the Pueblos' tight, complex social fabric with the Navahos' comparative individualism, the Pueblos' age-old self-sufficiency with the Navahos' cultural borrowings over the centuries—and asked themselves whether perhaps the old Pueblo virtues might not make adaptation the more difficult in a world now suddenly so changed from that desert environment to which the Pueblos were attuned. The Pueblos had taken on some surface coloring of non-Indian ways, the more readily because "they live in groups, communications are

Milton Snow—Navajo Service

easily realized, they were more in contact with Spanish
culture." But until recently they had seen no threat to
their deeply felt "integration with nature" or their "well-
structured social life." Any change in basic manner of life
or even in means of livelihood must be a challenge to
Pueblo beliefs. As one student wrote, "It is much easier
to bring electric wires to a row of small houses than to

install them in one great castle; the structure of the latter is too rigid."

In their reports the students stressed historical perspectives which might explain each tribe's situation and outlook. They wrote of class structures. They wrote of what similarities they found among the peoples visited, and what differences. They remarked repeatedly on inconsistencies: which "white" medicine a tribe might accept while at the same time rejecting other medical services; what endless hours a non-Indian doctor or nurse might work without complaint while at the same time refusing to respect patients. And again and again the students remarked on what must have seemed symbolic to Indians and Indian Service alike: the official requirement that a Hopi "come down from the mesa for whatever the Agency has to offer him" and in contrast the cooperation between the same Agency's doctors and the Hopi medicine men; the Government's belated success in getting Indians the vote, without the dire results some Pueblos feared, and on the other hand Pueblos Agency's mistake in nominating an Indian for federal jury duty before his neighbors could be sure no hurt would come:

"Reasoning from white experience, administrators seem to have believed that a chain reaction would develop in which other villagers would be anxious to follow the first juryman's lead and thus accumulate prestige. Instead, the result seems to be that he is hated."

There is no telling whether, as a result of the seminar, any given student matured differently from the way in which he would have anyway in one or another working experience. It did seem to the staff and to others who read

the student summaries that most of the students had matured in the five weeks of the seminar and were consequently the readier to learn from whatever jobs they might
undertake. Having known genuine cross-cultural contacts,
they could not be easily deceived by sham. They would,
surely, not be panicked by first failures. They had tried
their hands at practicing specific social sciences and specific
technical disciplines previously strange to them, and they
knew what sort of help they might seek from colleagues
in their effort to understand.

The seminar had suffered its own failures, nor could the
pressure of time excuse them all. As one student wisely
remarked (at the end of the fourth and last summer), he
could certainly have been provided a more extensive frame-
work of anthropological concepts at the start without dan-
ger that his own insights would be blurred.

Staff members were unsure at first just how much physical and intellectual strain the students could take. Although the first and smallest group of students responded
cheerfully to the rigors of visiting four communities, they
did flag noticeably toward the end of their run. The second year, the students were asked to study only three communities, and instead of living in Truchas they returned
each night to Santa Fe; apparently as a result, they never
did come as close to the people of Truchas as they had to
others.

One year, student recruitment was at fault. Too many
of the students were young, inexperienced, and without
specific points of view to contribute to their colleagues; to
make matters worse, these younger students had known
each other before coming to the seminar. Four had their

days of hanging back from the ever-new contacts in the seminar's race through the Southwest. Sometimes they seemed to feel that unless they could stride with magnificent assurance onto each new scene, they might as well stop trying to walk on-stage at all. Once again, the special failure that summer was at Truchas. There those four huddled together rather than risk the embarrassments of new contact. Going their rounds together, they found few villagers willing to talk with so many strangers at once. Or they listened in on someone else's interviews. Soon three of their colleagues were not sharing data but competing for it, and setting up a howl if others talked at all with any of "their" informants.

Finally, the seminar sometimes moved too quickly from area to area or from last visits to immediate faculty wrap-up. Granted that the seminar was set up for little more than a month and that the field trips, with travel time between, left barely a week for formal sessions at start and finish, still the students must have an honest day off after the Papago visit and after the Navaho visit and at least two days for talk among themselves after completing all three field trips. The days given to writing up notes on each area could not count as days off, important as the notes proved to sharp perception. Rest, too, was important, and again and again students came up with their shrewdest, broadest insights in moments when they were not required to think or talk, but did. And when, at the end of one seminar, faculty members lectured too soon on principles illustrated, they apparently disrupted the students' slower shaping of what *they* had seen and might articulate.

Ideally, such a seminar should last eight weeks or perhaps even ten. A first orientation period should be more leisurely than was possible in a five-week run; in it the many sorts of students may take their first hard look at one another, at least scan the "Suggested Reading" (which by and large they will not have dug into when a list is mailed them ahead of time), and perhaps even contemplate their lack of self-knowledge, their uncertainties about how they will measure up in the ordeal to come. For each week's concentrated work in and around one of the three communities visited, ten or eleven days should be allowed, to include setting up camp and report writing, a day off, and travel time. Finally, the students should have a period in which they may retrace their steps for further, detailed inquiry into any problem which has especially struck them. The writing of over-all reports should come after a few days of reflection. Faculty summaries—valuable as these are —should always be postponed until after faculty members have done all they can to help students bring to light their own conclusions.

Looking back, one faculty member, at least, could wish that the summers had been a little more different one from another. He, too, felt the pressure of time, yet it is his feeling now that he taught best when the problems and the ways of the peoples visited were new to him, as they were to the students. Perhaps the seminar should have gone more often where he, too, would be a stranger. Perhaps he should have shared more often that challenge of novelty which was the very essence of his students' experience.

John Collier, Jr.

Chapter 8

✖

New Windows on Alien Worlds

The seminar described in these pages built on familiar training procedures. Such pioneers as Boas and Lowie and Kroeber undertook their own first great anthropological researches plunging into unknown communities alone— and sent their students to do likewise. Many anthropologists have taken groups of students into the field to train them in research methods. The Foreign Service Institute has taught civil servants both to incorporate social science into their perspectives on specific community problems and to look into their own characteristics as Americans. Learning by doing and social learning are hardly new educational concepts. The Cornell seminar in cross-cultural relations combined such known methods of teaching—and added its own stress on the kaleidoscopic.

Although the success of the seminar would seem to have depended largely on what range of experience individual students could contribute to the shared analysis, and although it might perhaps be argued that such students must

John Collier, Jr.

almost inevitably achieve a sense of fellowship and a re-
alization of the diversity of the problems of cross-cultural
relationships, it would seem that the quick turns from one
community to another were valuable not merely to prevent
facile conclusions about "native peoples in general," but
also to bring out the different students' very different perceptions. Then too, the rigors of their jaunting added to
the students' sense of their own community. When they
found themselves back in a conventional classroom, at the

Santa Fe Indian School, that classroom seemed somehow strange, alive with what they had seen together, lit by new windows looking out on alien worlds. In their final discussions, they found themselves glancing back on what they had seen through one another's eyes.

They were indebted to one another, too, for the details that had suddenly illuminated, such as the thirty-year-old letter a Navaho had dug from his trunk and shown the Hawaiian student. "Build up your flock," a government agent had written the Navaho. "Your future is in sheep."

They were indebted to one another for cross-lighting, as when one American girl suddenly saw Papago successes and failures in the perspective gained from the Bolivian's tale of a farm cooperative near his home. (That cooperative accomplished nothing until someone thought to ask the farmers what else they wanted to do cooperatively besides plan and buy and sell; they answered, "Play music, have a band.")

They were indebted as well for over-all attitudes. The Asian agriculturalists, for example, were impressed by American students' pitching into manual labor. The students were indebted for what men and women of other skills and disciplines had taught them about alternate, perhaps more promising, bridges for cross-cultural communication.

If they remembered the frustration of the individual Navaho baffled by government policies on stock reduction as something they had somehow experienced personally, they did so very largely because a few of them had already known and felt strongly about how uncertainties may plague farmer or rancher. If one summer's students vividly recalled a Pueblo farmer who had forgotten that government can be more than a handout, more than just somebody else's responsibility, they did so because the psychologist among them dug deeper into that farmer's conflicting, never-reconciled values.

If a routine Papago Council meeting, conducted almost entirely in the native tongue, had seemed to dramatize Papago foresight and enthusiasm and vigor, the students may have gained this sense from the fact that one of their number had talked all night long with a Papago leader, in shared excitement over the detailed workings of representative government. And when another, through his own exhaustive inspections, was able to demonstrate to his fellows what ingenuity Papagos exercise in their water use,

John Collier, Jr.

they had come to appreciate not only Papago ways and desert water problems, but a friend's insights and perspectives.

Because one of the students, with extraordinary human warmth and an interest in human difference, felt especially close to "his" Truchas family, some of the others found their own potential warmth and interest so stirred as to feel that their friend's experience was theirs as well. And having stumbled in on the hilarity of a Navaho rodeo or climbed down to the white sands and green gardens of that fairyland which is Canyon de Chelly, they had shared one another's capacity for wonder and joy. Although these students lost touch with one another, alumni of similar programs run by any one governmental bureau for its own employees might well continue to share ideas and experiences on the job.

Perhaps the faculty members' main contribution, aside from plain logistics, was to keep such students perceiving their own learning process. They contributed, first, the firm refusal to tell students "how to interview." They contributed, throughout, a stress on what must be learned and relearned about peoples living, suffering, and aspiring, rather than on what set characteristics these peoples exhibit. They contributed such an ordering of problems, each more complex than the preceding, that the students could sense and apply their own new skills. They contributed that matter-of-fact acceptance of specific failures necessary if those who fail—whole nations, indeed—are not to wallow in a sense of being ill-adapted, unwanted.

Such training as the seminar afforded should perhaps go especially to top-level administrators. What they learn (or are reminded that they already know) may so inform their work as to seep down to their colleagues. In addition, they themselves may need to go back and "touch first." Culture can be a tyrant. Our own set ways of looking at what we may consider the set ways of strangers may prevent us from really seeing the peoples we encounter. Administrators may need help in regaining their freshness of vision when they look up from their budget memoranda. They may need

John Collier, Jr.

the reminder that they have forgotten how to share food,
how to talk with the man on the unpaved street, how to see
the close relationships between peoples and their lands.
They may need new windows on what would otherwise be
alien worlds indeed.

—